Cheetah Cubs and Beetle Grubs

The Wacky Ways We Name Young Animals

Text by Diane Swanson

Illustrations by Mariko Ando Spencer

annick press
toronto + new york + vancouver

Full of fun, young mountain goats are **KiDS**—just like you. They spend a lot of time playing games, such as Follow the Leader. They also climb on rocks, then try to knock one another off. The strongest kid gets to be the leader.

Mountain Goat KiDS

neat to know

- Being born on steep cliffs helps mountain goat kids avoid predators such as wolves.
- Bumpy, rubberlike pads on the bottoms of their hooves help the kids avoid slipping.
- Both male and female mountain goat kids grow horns that they never shed.

- One mouse pinkie weighs no more than two mini-marshmallows.
- It takes mouse pinkies just 10 days to grow coats of white or gray-brown fur.
- Mouse pinkies can sense sounds that are too high-pitched for you to hear.

Mouse Pinkies

With pink, hairless skin, newborn house mice are **Pinkies**. But they're shorter than a man's smallest fingers—his pinkies. When female house mice are only 10 weeks old, they can give birth to pinkies of their own.

- A keen sense of smell helps mackerel spikes find food.
- Thousands of mackerel spikes gather together in schools.
- As mackerel spikes grow, they can swim even faster than speedy predators such as swordfish.

Mackerel Spikes

Young mackerel called **spikes** are a lot like tent spikes. They're both narrow and about 15 centimeters (6 inches) long. They're shiny and metallic in color. And if some kinds of mackerel spikes stop swimming, they sink.

Just like rumba dancers, young mosquitoes are **wigglers**. They hurl their bodies side to side, wiggling with almost every move. Even to catch a breath of air, young mosquitoes wiggle up to the water's surface.

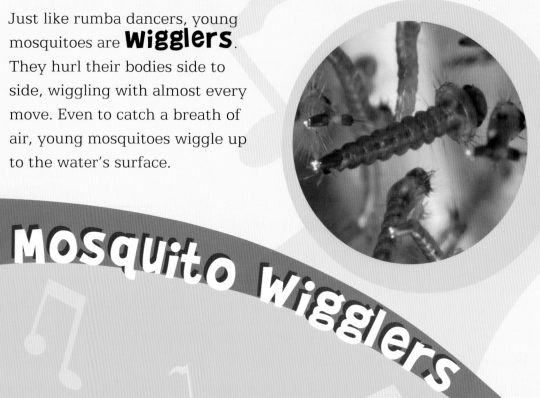

Mosquito Wigglers

Neat to know

- Mosquito wigglers can live in water trapped in a tree hole.
- Most mosquito wigglers feed on tiny bits of plants, but some eat other wigglers.
- By shaking hairs on their heads, mosquito wigglers make food float right to them.

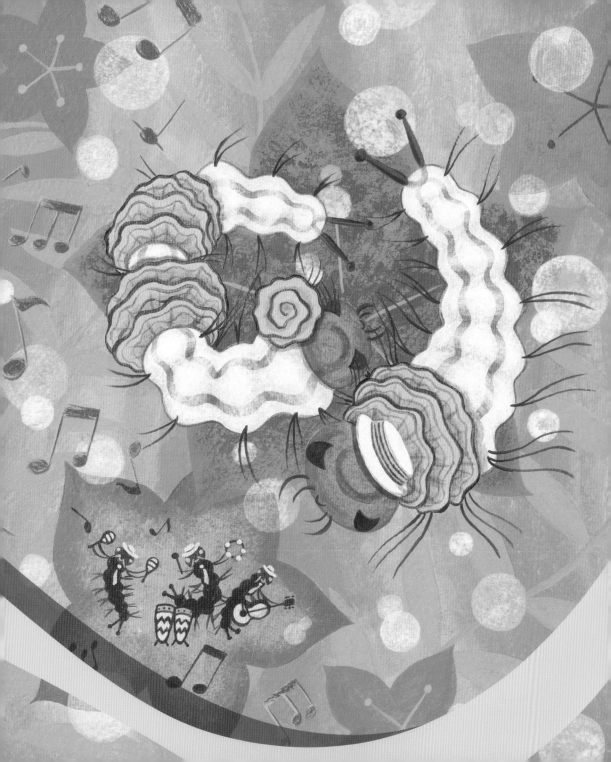

- When canvasback flappers master flying, these ducks can travel faster than cars zoom down a highway.
- Some mallard flappers start life in nests built in balcony flowerpots.
- American black flappers learn to take off from water by rising straight up.

Duck Flappers

Fluttering their wings constantly, young ducks are **flappers**. They're a bit like flappers of the 1920s— young women who spent lots of energy dancing, just as duck flappers do while they're learning to fly.

- At birth, a cheetah cub weighs only as much as a large apple.
- The eyes of newborn cheetahs stay closed for one to two weeks.
- Cheetah cubs learn to run fast. As adults, they're the swiftest mammals on Earth.

Cheetah CUBS

Young cheetahs are **CUBS**. Like Cub Scouts, they learn outdoor skills from grown-ups. They wrestle one another, climb trees, and play tug-of-war. And they're great at hiding. Cheetah cubs blend well in shadows and tall grass.

Common food for bears, raccoons, and skunks, young beetles—called **GRUBS**—make good eating. Pawfuls of the thick, wormlike grubs pack as much protein as the beans and stews cowboys ate on the range.

Beetle Grubs

neat to know

- Tiger beetle grubs hide in burrows and grab prey that pass by.
- Young ladybugs are beetle grubs with huge appetites. One can eat 500 aphids in a day.
- Unlike most other insects, giant carrion beetles make fine parents. They look after their grubs.

- As they grow, pigeon squeakers use the position of the sun to help them find their way.
- By sucking up water with their beaks, pigeon squeakers learn to drink.
- Pigeon squeakers can easily hear far-off thunderstorms.

Pigeon squeakers

Young pigeons are **squeakers**, especially at feeding times. Like rubber toys, they make high-pitched squeaks over and over again. Fast-growing squeakers are almost always hungry—and squeaking—when they're learning to eat grain.

Sometimes young eels are called **flies**. They're small like the flies, or lures, that people tie to lines on their fishing rods. And both kinds of flies attract many fish that try to snap them up as food.

Eel Flies

neat to know

- Even older, bigger eels chase and eat little eel flies.
- When many gray eel flies swim together, they can make a stream look gray.
- Eel flies can leave the water and wriggle over damp moss to get past powerful waterfalls.

- Skunk kits learn to catch fish by watching their mothers.
- If they must, skunk kits can swim for hours at a time.
- Skunk kits often play by splashing water on one another.

skunk Kits

Young skunks are **kits**, like gardening kits. They both come with work gloves and digging tools. The thick skin on a skunk kit's front paws acts like a pair of gloves—even preventing wasp stings. And its sharp claws are great for digging.

Thousands of young salmon, called **fry**, are like a giant food fry—a picnic for people. Both groups meet outdoors in large numbers, and they stuff themselves with food. As salmon fry swim toward the sea, they gobble all the insects they can.

Salmon Fry

neat to know

- Only one of every five salmon eggs might survive to become a fry.
- When salmon fry begin searching for food, they're just half as long as your thumb.
- Large insects can snap up small salmon fry.

Text © 2007 Diane Swanson
Illustrations © 2007 Mariko Ando Spencer
Photography: cover top, © istockphoto.com; cover bottom, © istockphoto.com/Chris Fourie; mountain goats, © Sumio Harada/First Light; mice, © E.R. Degginger/First Light; mackerel, Crown copyright, Fisheries Research Services, photograph taken by TG Mcinnes; mosquito larvae, © Paul Davidson, reprinted with permission; duck, © Skara Froggy, www.sxc.hu, reprinted with permission; cheetahs, © Daniel Cox/First Light; beetle grub, © istockphoto.com; pigeons, © Heidi & Hans-Jurgen Koch/First Light; eels, © Heather Angel/Natural Visions; skunks, © Konrad Wothe/First Light; salmon, © Flip Nicklin/First Light.

Annick Press Ltd.

We acknowledge the support of the Canada Council for the Arts, the Ontario Arts Council, and the Government of Canada through the Book Publishing Industry Development Program (BPIDP) for our publishing activities.

Edited by Elizabeth McLean
Cover and interior design by Maggie Woo and Ivy Lee/Daniel Choi Design

Cataloguing in Publication
Swanson, Diane, 1944–
    Cheetah cubs and beetle grubs : the wacky ways we name young animals / text by Diane Swanson ; illustrations by Mariko Ando Spencer.

ISBN-13: 978-1-55451-084-9 (bound)
ISBN-10: 1-55451-084-8 (bound)
ISBN-13: 978-1-55451-083-2 (pbk.)
ISBN-10: 1-55451-083-X (pbk.)

    1. Animals—Nomenclature (Popular)—Juvenile literature.
2. Animals—Infancy—Juvenile literature. I. Spencer, Mariko Ando
II. Title.

QL49.S923 2007   j591.3'9014   C2007-900688-4

The text was typeset in Antique and Brady Bunch.
The art was rendered in watercolor.

Printed and bound in China

Published in the U.S.A. by
Annick Press (U.S.) Ltd.

Distributed in Canada by
Firefly Books Ltd.
66 Leek Crescent
Richmond Hill, ON
L4B 1H1

Distributed in the U.S.A. by
Firefly Books (U.S.) Inc.
P.O. Box 1338
Ellicott Station
Buffalo, NY 14205

Visit our website at **www.annickpress.com**